LASER BASICS

by **Lawrence Stevens**

Drawings by
Art Seiden

With Photographs

Created and Produced by
Arvid Knudsen

Prentice-Hall Books for Young Readers
A Division of Simon & Schuster, Inc.
New York

DEDICATION:

To my son, Jamie Lee

Other **High-Tech Basics** Books in Series
COMPUTER BASICS *by Hal Hellman*
VIDEO BASICS *by J. T. Yurko*
HOME COMPUTER BASICS *by Jeffrey Rothfeder*
PHOTOGRAPHY BASICS *by Vick Owens-Knudsen*
COMPUTER PROGRAMMING BASICS *by Lawrence Stevens*
ELECTRONICS BASICS *by Carl Laron*
COMPUTER GRAPHICS BASICS *by Lawrence Stevens*
MONEY BASICS *by G. David Wallace*
COMPUTER SOFTWARE BASICS *by Carl Laron*
ROBOTICS BASICS *by Karen Liptak*
WORD PROCESSING BASICS *by Art Dudley*
LASER BASICS *by Lawrence Stevens*

Text copyright © 1985 by Lawrence Stevens and
Arvid Knudsen
Illustrations copyright © 1985 by Arvid Knudsen
All rights reserved including the right of
reproduction in whole or in part in any form.
Published by Prentice-Hall Books for Young Readers
A Division of Simon & Schuster, Inc.
Simon & Schuster Building
Rockefeller Center
1230 Avenue of the Americas
New York, NY 10020

10 9 8 7 6 5 4 3 2

Prentice-Hall Books for Young Readers
is a trademark of Simon & Schuster, Inc.
Manufactured in the United States of America
Designed by Arvid Knudsen

Library of Congress Cataloging in Publication Data
Stevens, Lawrence.
  Laser basics.
  Summary: Discusses the development and uses of
the laser, a tool increasingly utilized in medicine,
the military, manufacturing, and other diverse fields.
  1. Lasers—Juvenile literature. [1. Lasers]
I. Seiden, Art, ill. II. Knudsen, Arvid. III. Title.
TA1682.S74 1985   621.36′6   85-9408
ISBN 0-13-523606-1

CONTENTS

Photo Credits:
Pps. 10, 17, 19 and 20 courtesy of Coherent, Inc.
P. 14 courtesy of Eye Research Institute of America
Pps. 28 and 32 courtesy of American Banknote Co., Inc.
P. 40 courtesy of Sony Corporation of America

1 | Unleashing the Power of Light

In 1898, H.G. Wells wrote a novel called *The War of the Worlds*. In this book, the earth was attacked by Martians and almost defeated by their terrible weapon: a machine that shot deadly light rays. This "ghost of a beam of light" was able to blast through brick houses, set forests on fire, and cut through metal.

In the 1930s, comic-strip space warrior Buck Rogers used a ray gun to defeat alien enemies.

The idea of light having enough force to cut, pierce, blast, and fire is not new to science fiction writers. But it wasn't until the summer of 1960 that the world got its first glimpse of this awesome power.

That summer, a thirty-three-year-old engineer named Theodore H. Maiman showed the world a four-inch tube that contained a ruby rod encircled by a flash tube. It was an innocent looking device, but when he turned it on, a light flashed from it that outshone the sun. The power that Maiman released is strong enough to cut through diamonds, hot enough to weld metal, and destructive enough to shoot down rockets. And yet it is so controllable, a surgeon can direct the beam into a patient's eye without injuring healthy tissue. Or it can help to perform such everyday tasks as reading bar codes on groceries or playing video and audio discs.

This light is called a laser, and many scientists believe that it is the most important discovery of the century. One Japanese government official predicted that lasers will change our lives more than the steam engine and the harnessing of electricity.

◀ COMIC STRIPS AND SCIENCE FICTION HAVE LONG ANTICIPATED THE LASER AND HOLOGRAMS.

Courtesy of Peter Pan Books and Records, Inc.
Amazing Adventures of Holoman.
Permission by Donald Kasen, co-creator.

THE ORDINARY LIGHT BULB
CASTS IT'S LIGHT IN WAVES
ALL OVER.

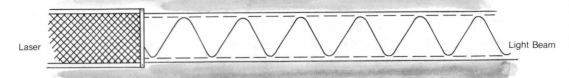

Laser

Light Beam

THE LASER FOCUSES LIGHTWAVES IN A THIN, POWERFUL STRAIGHT LINE.

Although the exact way a laser works is very complicated, the concept is really very simple. It is based on the principle that light can heat things. We know that sunlight can warm us, even on a cold day. And many of us have filtered sunlight through a magnifying glass to set dry leaves on fire (don't try this, though, without adult supervision).

Sunlight can do this because it is very powerful. How can earthly light be strengthened so that it is even brighter and more powerful than sunlight? The answer lies partly in the laser's ability to focus light through a very small area.

To understand this, hold a piece of paper up to a desk lamp. The light that hits the paper is pretty bright. That is because light is made up of waves, like the waves of the ocean. When the paper is near the lamp, it receives almost all of the light waves. But as you move the paper away from the lamp, the paper receives fewer waves and is less bright. A laser focuses most of the waves from a light into one very thin, very powerful line.

Another way to picture this is to think of water coming out of a garden hose. If the hose opening is not obstructed, the water may come out slowly. But cover part of the opening with your thumb and the water

WHEN A PIECE OF PAPER IS HELD NEAR A LAMP, THE PAPER RECEIVES MOST OF THE LIGHT WAVES, AND IT BECOMES BRIGHT. AS THE PAPER IS MOVED FROM THE LAMP, FEWER LIGHT WAVES HIT IT, AND IT BECOMES LESS BRIGHT.

will come out with much more force. That is because you are squeezing the same amount of water through a smaller opening. Lasers get their strength from concentrating light waves into a very small area.

Lasers have another quality that makes them stronger than ordinary light. If you filter ordinary sunlight or lamplight through a prism, you will see a rainbow of colors. This is because white light contains waves of many different lengths; each length is seen as a different color. But laser light comes in only one wavelength. This makes it much more powerful. It is a little like an army of soldiers marching together. That would make a much more powerful force than a ragtag crowd of men, women, and children.

THE LASER BEAM HAS A FANTASTIC POTENTIAL USE IN COMMUNICATIONS AND OTHER APPLICATIONS BECAUSE OF THE HIGH COHERENCE PROPERTY IN THE BEAM WHICH MAKES IT CONTROLLABLE.

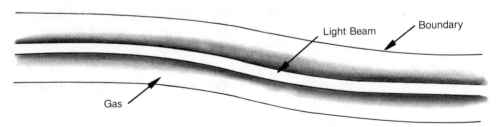

Light Beam

Boundary

Gas

IN A PIPE THAT CURVES THE GAS ACTS LIKE A PRISM, DEFLECTING THE LASER BEAM IN THE DIRECTION OF THE CURVE.

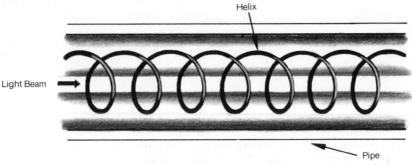

THE HELICAL CONVECTION GAS LENS.

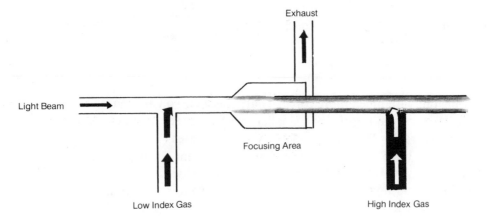

THE COUNTER-FLOWING GAS LENS.

The word *laser* is an acronym. An acronym is a word that is made up of the first letters of other words. *Laser* stands for Light Amplification by Stimulated Emission of Radiation. Amplification means "to make larger or stronger," and we already know that lasers make light stronger.

To understand what "stimulated emission of radiation" is, we have to know a little bit about atoms. Everything in the visible universe is made up of atoms: water, paper, planets, stars, even air. Each atom has three parts: neutrons, protons, and electrons. Neutrons and protons stay in the center, or nucleus, of the atom, but electrons circle around the nucleus like planets circling around a sun.

Some atoms are like close-knit families. Their electrons like nothing better than to stay home and circle around their nucleus. Other atoms have electrons that are very excitable. They are always looking for an opportunity to run away from home and join another family of atoms.

A laser tube contains a material that has excitable electrons. These are stimulated (the *S* in laSer) in some way, and they begin to move around wildly. But very quickly they settle down, and as they do, each one emits a tiny burst of light energy called a photon. A photon is a unit of light. Photons are what tans us in the sun and toasts bread. If photos were easily released from some laser tubes, they could do little more than burn toast. But in the laser tube are two mirrors. Most of the photons are trapped as they bounce back and forth between those mirrors. And as they do, they stimulate other electrons to emit more photons. As the photons continue their back-and-forth trips, they grow in number. At first only a few photons are bouncing back and forth, then thousands, then millions. Within less than one second, an uncountable number of photons fill the tube and align themselves, ready to burst out of the tube as a needle of radiation, or laser light—a light so powerful that it can only be described as unearthly.

In this book, we will look at the many uses of this light force. We will find surgeons using it in place of knives. We will see how it is used in factories in place of cutting and drilling tools. We will learn of plans to use it in warfare: to shoot down rockets, to aim artillery, and to confuse enemy radar. We will see how it is used in communication and navigation. And we will find out about light shows against the sky and three-dimensional images that seem to float in midair.

Laser research is still very young. Hundreds of ideas of how to use this power have been proposed. But so far only a few have been put into actual use. And yet it is likely that in a few years, so many aspects of human life will be affected by lasers that it may be called the light of the twenty-first century.

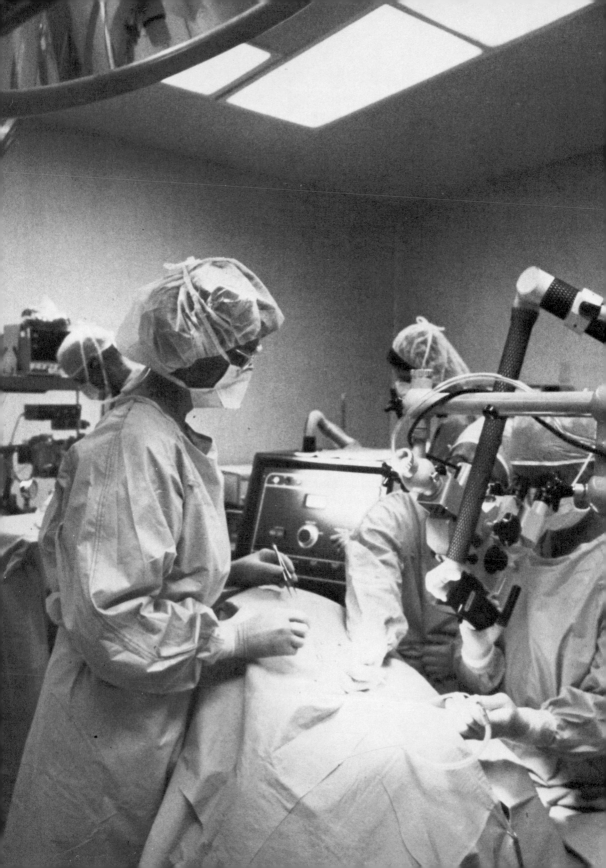

2 | Lasers in Medicine

A third grade schoolteacher in Chicago, Illinois, noticed one day that her voice was a bit hoarse. Thinking that it might have resulted from yelling at a student during recess, she ignored it. But the hoarseness didn't improve the next day or even the next week. In fact, it got worse every day. When it got so bad that her students had trouble hearing her, she decided to go to her doctor.

The doctor discovered that lumps had formed on her larynx, or voice box. These lumps, also called tumors, were not cancerous, but as they grew they were beginning to choke off her voice. So they had to be removed. Normally, that operation would have to be performed with a sharp knife called a scalpel. After the operation, her throat would be very sore and she wouldn't be able to talk for many weeks.

Luckily, a new way of performing this operation was available. The surgeon directed a laser beam into her throat. The beam burned out the tumor without hurting the area around it. So a few days after the operation, she was talking in her normal voice.

In Collier County, Florida, a grandfather loved to go on hikes with his three grandchildren. Behind his house were miles of wooded trails where the four of them could pick blueberries, wade in streams, sometimes catch sight of a colorful snake, or learn the names of trees. One year though, that all ended.

LASER SURGERY IN HOSPITALS IS
BECOMING ALMOST ROUTINE.

Grandfather's right leg had begun to hurt so badly he could barely walk. Even when he rested, the pain was sometimes so bad that he could not enjoy playing cards with his grandchildren. The doctors said that one of his arteries—a blood vessel that brought blood to his leg—was clogged with a fatty deposit. He had two operations but both were unsuccessful. The only way to relieve the pain was to amputate, or cut off, his leg. So he went to a hospital to have it done.

But while he was there, a surgeon told him about a new type of operation that might remove the fatty deposit without removing the leg. A special tiny wire would be slipped into his artery like slipping a thread through a straw. The wire would be snaked up the artery until it got to the fatty deposit. A laser beam then would be shot out of the wire. If successful, this would burn up the deposit.

It worked! A day later, he was out of the hospital with just a Band-Aid on his leg. His leg no longer hurt him. And in a short while, he and his grandchildren could again enjoy their walks through the woods.

Lasers are beginning to be used to treat many medical problems that could not be treated before. They can remove large, red "port wine" birthmarks, they can stop bleeding, and even help in reattaching limbs that were cut off in an accident. But the most common and oldest use of lasers in medicine is to treat certain eye diseases.

Gayle is an eighth-grader in New York City. She is close to the top of her class in reading and history. Last year, she won the state-wide spelling bee, and this year she was tied for second in a contest to see which student could read the most books in two months. But something happened to her that forced her to cut down on the amount of her reading.

One day as she was copying some notes off a chalkboard, a light flashed in front of her eyes. Then the light seemed to stay in front of her sight, blocking her vision. Later, she began to see black specks that seemed to fall down like soot from a chimney. Those specks bothered her whenever she tried to read.

Her doctor explained to her that part of her retina, the back of her eye, had ripped. This caused the light to flash. A little blood also had leaked out, and that is what caused the black specks.

The doctor explained that the eyeball had a thick outer shell, like a tennis ball. In front of the eye is a transparent window called the cornea. The cornea allows the image of what you are seeing to enter the eye. That

LASER SET-UP FOR EYE SURGERY.

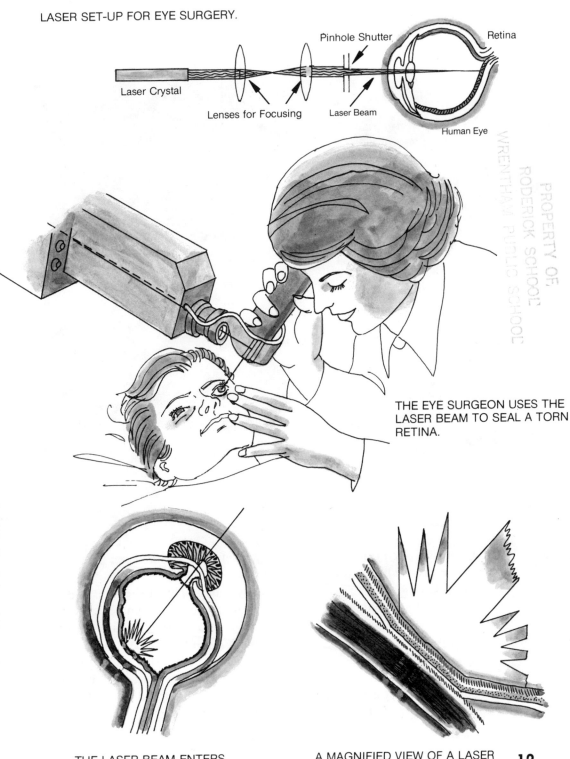

Pinhole Shutter

Retina

Laser Crystal

Lenses for Focusing

Laser Beam

Human Eye

THE EYE SURGEON USES THE LASER BEAM TO SEAL A TORN RETINA.

THE LASER BEAM ENTERS THROUGH THE PUPIL OF THE EYE AND MAKES CONTACT WITH A TINY AREA OF THE RETINA.

A MAGNIFIED VIEW OF A LASER BEAM ACTUALLY WELDING RETINA TO UNDERLYING STRUCTURE.

13

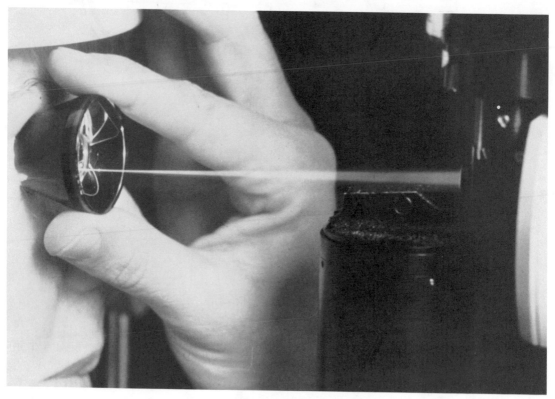

LASER OPERATION IN PROGRESS.

image is projected onto the retina, which sends it to the brain. The brain then interprets what you are seeing.

Most times when people go to an eye doctor, he or she examines the retina. The doctor shines a light through the cornea and then peeks in. But it is not easy for a doctor to see tears or rips in the retina because they are very tiny—smaller than the head of a pin. It is a little like peeking through a keyhole into a dark room and trying to read a handwritten note hanging on a far wall. For that reason, some doctors use a very weak laser to illuminate the area. It is much brighter than ordinary light and so it allows the doctor to use more magnification when examining the retina.

After the examination, the doctor explained to Gayle and her parents that her condition was very serious. Very often, a few weeks or months after the retina tears, it breaks off completely. If that happened, Gayle would have a curtain on the side of her vision. She might feel that she is always looking through a tunnel. Or if the retina becomes detached in the center of her vision, her sight might seem blurred, as if she were looking through water.

A few years ago, there would have been little hope for Gayle. Now lasers are used to repair torn retinas. A powerful but very thin beam is sent through the cornea until it hits the retina. The beam does not hurt the cornea, but it burns the retina and welds it back to the eye. It also forms tiny scars that stop the leaking of blood.

Gayle was very nervous when she went to have her laser surgery. But she kept remembering what her doctor told her: "The operation probably will not hurt at all. We will put a contact lens on your eye, but nothing will be inserted into your eye. You will be awake throughout the operation, and when it is over you can get up and go home."

Gayle was shown a room that had a machine that she was asked to look into. A nurse held her head firmly to keep her from moving. The doctor looked into the other end of the machine and asked her to look directly at a light. Then Gayle saw a bright light that was very uncomfortable but did not hurt at all. She knew that light was the laser beam, but since there are no pain cells in the retina, she did not feel it burning. When it was over, just as the doctor promised, she got up and went home with her parents.

The operation worked. Soon after, Gayle's vision improved quite a bit. She was able to read, play, and watch TV almost as well as she did before.

Laser surgery is called unintrusive. That means the operation is done without cutting the patient. Some doctors feel that people in the future will think present scalpel methods of surgery are pitifully backward, just as we now disdain the older methods of bleeding patients with leeches and performing operations with dirty hands.

3 | Lasers in Industry: Light Beams at Work

Have you ever visited a factory such as those that manufacture automobiles, clothes, or metal parts? If you have, you may have seen a place that was dirty, noisy, and hot.

Maybe you saw an assembly line. As the part being worked on moves along a conveyor belt, workers drill holes, cut patterns, tighten screws, or do some other job.

When the part passes through the drilling station, a worker lowers a drill that screeches loudly as it cuts into the metal. The sound seems to set your teeth on edge, and the dust and shavings from the hole fill the air and then float to the floor.

Another worker uses a cutting blade. It does not screech like the drill; rather, it seems to yell. The noise is almost deafening. And you know if you were not wearing a face mask, the dust from the cutting would get into your lungs and make you cough.

Another worker is wearing a metal helmet that looks a little like a medieval knight's face mask. He uses a torch to weld pieces of metal together. You have to stand far back from him, and you are warned not to look at the flame. You are too far back to feel any heat from the torch. But you know that the three welding stations in the factory are adding to the intense heat. It feels as if it is over 100 degrees in there. You are soaked with sweat. And the noise and dirt are giving you a headache. You enjoy watching how the factory works. But you also are happy when your tour is over and you can breathe some cool, crisp air.

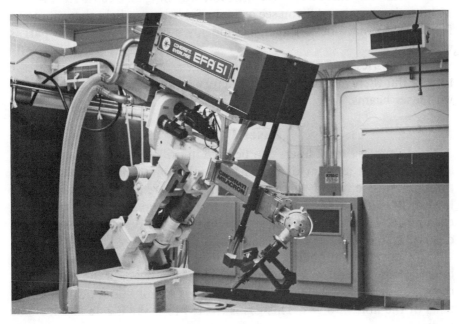

A LASER DRILL.

Of course, all factories are not this bad. Many have special devices that cut down on noise, dirt, and heat. And others have robots doing many of the jobs. That cuts down on the number of people in the factory, but robots and mechanical arms add to the noise with their vibrating clatter.

One way to provide a cleaner, quieter, faster, and even cooler factory would be to use lasers to perform many of the jobs now done by other machines. We already have seen that lasers can cut, bore holes, and heat to high temperatures. So it is possible for them to replace saws, drills, and welding torches.

Let's look at how a laser factory would operate.

The part that is being worked on still moves along a conveyor belt. But that is all that moves. There are no loud machines. And there are no robots, mechanical arms, or humans moving around, stirring up dust and making a racket. Instead, as the part moves across a work station, a laser beam hits it at just the right spot. The beam is silent as it bores a hole, cuts through metal, or welds parts together.

Watching this factory is a little like watching an electric storm—but without the thunder. All you see are colorful beams of light that shoot out from distant machines. And then suddenly a hole is drilled or a part is welded.

Factories that use lasers for all their operations are still in the future. But there are already many factory tasks that are being performed with laser beams.

Laser Drilling

Even very weak lasers can be used in drilling. A forty-watt laser—about the same amount of light as a weak table lamp—can easily drill through ceramic, wood, plastic, or cloth. But there are also very powerful laser drills. These are called heavy lasers, and they may have 4,000 watts or even more. They may be used for drilling heavy pipes, auto parts, or industrial diamonds.

Conventional nonlaser drills work by rotating a bit so fast that it bores a hole. To drill with a laser, you aim a laser beam of the right size at the spot where the hole is needed. The light is so hot that it turns the contents of the hole into gas. This gas is treated to make it safe and it floats away.

Here are some reasons why laser drills are better than conventional drills:

1. *Laser drills make almost no mess. When using conventional drills, the material from the hole usually fills the air and then floats to the floor. With a laser, the contents of the hole are vaporized (turned into gas).*

2. *A laser can be computer-programmed to make a hole of any size. This eliminates the need to keep changing the size of the drill bit.*

3. *Although lasers are hot, they work so fast that they actually send less heat to the area around the hole than a conventional drill. This helps prevent cracking.*

4. *Lasers can make tiny holes in just the right place. For that reason, they often are used to drill watch parts or the tiny ceramic chips that are the "brains" of computers.*

5. *Lasers also can drill holes in very soft surfaces without damaging the rest of the part. So they often are used to drill holes in spray (aerosol) container nozzles and nipples for baby bottles.*

18

LASER DRILLS CAN DRILL THROUGH CERAMIC, WOOD, PLASTIC,
CLOTH AND HEAVIER DRILLS MAY BE USED FOR DRILLING HEAVY
PIPES, AUTO PARTS AND INDUSTRIAL DIAMONDS.

LASER CUTTING STATION.

6. *Laser beams can get into difficult-to-reach places more easily than conventional drills. So they often are used to drill holes in pipes and tubes.*

7. *Lasers are useful in drilling only half way through something. Since the content of the hole is vaporized, there is no dust to be cleaned out.*

Laser Cutting

Conventional cutting may be performed with a grinding wheel or a saw blade. In a factory, the cutting station is usually the noisiest. Grinding stones and blades vibrate and rumble. And they bring up mounds of dust. They also wear out quickly. It is not only expensive to replace blades so often, but it also takes time and slows up production.

A laser beam is silent and it never wears out. It also is cleaner since it turns the cut edge into liquid instead of dust.

Recently, a British company developed a laser that automatically cuts fabric into parts of clothing. An operator provides the laser's computer with information about the style of the clothes, the number of pieces desired, and the sizes. After that information is programmed into the computer, the fabric travels along a conveyor belt in front of the laser. The laser beam automatically, silently, and quickly cuts the right patterns.

Laser Welding

Welding is the process of fusing, or attaching, two things together with heat. Very simply, the two parts being attached are heated, joined, and then cooled. The result is that the two parts become one. It is one of the strongest bonds available.

Conventional welding is a complicated, messy, and expensive process. It may involve special rods, chemicals, and protective material in the area around the weld. Laser welding, on the other hand, is much simpler. The laser beam simply heats the correct areas on both parts and they are attached. The intense laser heat makes chemicals that are needed in conventional welding unnecessary. And the process is so fast that there is little danger of the area around the weld being affected.

4 | Lasers at War: The Dark Side of the Force

Almost as soon as the laser was invented, scientists began thinking about how it could be used in warfare. And on March 23, 1983, President Ronald Reagan, in a speech, gave his support to a weapons system that would make heavy use of lasers. Some people called it the "Star Wars" plan because it entailed sending weapons into space. But the President prefers to call it his strategic defense initiative.

The part of the speech that stunned the nation and even surprised many scientists was when President Reagan asked "the scientific community in our country . . . to turn their great talents now to the cause of mankind and world peace; to give us the means of rendering these nuclear weapons impotent and obsolete. . . ."

In other words, the President was asking scientists to figure out a way to stop nuclear weapons that might be launched from hitting the earth. If this could happen, countries would no longer have to spend money building these terrible weapons, and the world would no longer be afraid of them because they would be useless.

The President's plan calls for the development and use of laser weapons to act as guns to shoot down missiles. Presently, no country has a way of preventing nuclear weapons from hitting its land. Nuclear war is prevented by fear of retaliation. This is called mutually assured destruction, which means that each side knows that if it attacks the other, it also would be attacked.

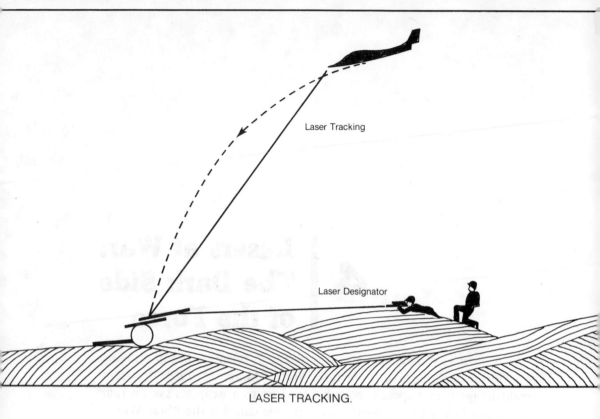

LASER TRACKING.

People who support the President's plan say that every country has the right and duty to defend itself. Since at present we have no real defense against in-coming missiles, we are not fulfilling that duty. Without laser weapons, shooting down a large number of missiles would be impossible. Now that we are close to developing laser weapon systems, the President's supporters say we have a responsibility to put them into use. Some supporters also argue that an antimissile system would mean the end of nuclear weapons. And that once we develop it, we should give the plans to the entire world so that everyone would be free of danger.

But those who are against the strategic defense initiative say that such a system would be too expensive to build, and that it would not be able to stop all the in-coming missiles anyway. They also argue that while the system was being built, the Soviet Union probably would figure out a way to defeat it. So all the time and money spent on the project would have been wasted.

But whatever side you take, it is interesting to see how these weapons would work. But first it is important to understand why lasers would be necessary in such a weapons system.

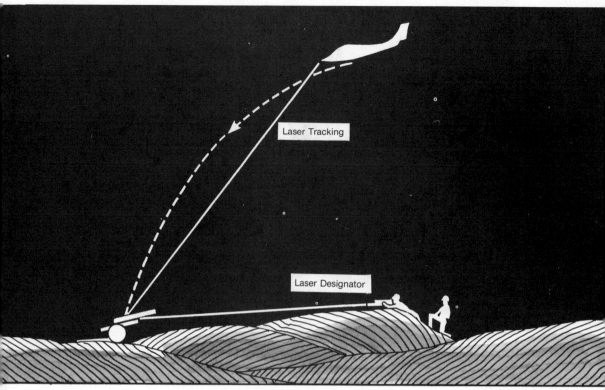

GROUND LASER DESIGNATOR TRACKING.

Knocking out a guided missile before it lands is a lot like hitting a bullet with a bullet. A guided missile can reach this country from the Soviet Union in less than half an hour. It is as fast as a bullet; and when it is far away, it might seem almost as small as a bullet. Hitting such a small moving object with another missile is very difficult. This is not to say it cannot be done, but it presents problems that would not exist with the much faster, more accurate laser beam.

Another problem is that once an attack of, say, 5,000 missiles was launched, there probably also would be a launch of tens of thousands of decoy balloons. These decoys would confuse the missiles that were sent to destroy the real weapons. The only solution would be to shoot out the missiles as they are being launched. But the launch takes only about 100 seconds. Even if we had missiles in space aimed at the enemy's launch sites and we fired as soon as they launched their rockets, our missiles would arrive on target too late. A laser, though, travels at the speed of light, or 186,000 miles per second. It would take less than a second for a laser beam to reach the enemy missiles.

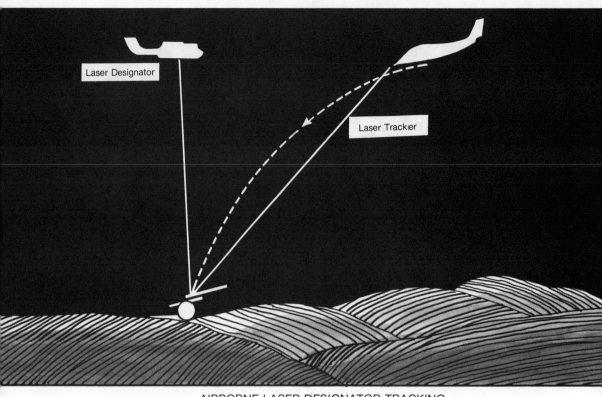

AIRBORNE LASER DESIGNATOR TRACKING.

The laser that would be orbiting in space would be much larger and more powerful than any built so far. The mirrors in most lasers are less than an inch in diameter; the ones in these weapons might be close to thirty-five yards in diameter. A strong industrial laser might be 10,000 watts strong; this weapon would be well over a million watts. All lasers need some power source to excite their electrons. The power source in a space laser weapon would be a small nuclear explosion. This nuclear explosion would be magnified by the laser from 1,000 times to as high as 100,000 times.

The lasers used for this system can be of basically two types:

A *pulsed laser* delivers short but very powerful bursts of power. This would not destroy the missile but it would knock it off course. The missile would then wander forever through space.

A *continuous-wave laser* would stay on the target until it bored a hole into it. The missile then would explode harmlessly in space.

These orbiting laser weapons may never become a reality. But there are other military uses of lasers that are now being used or that surely will be put to use soon.

For example, in a test performed in 1976, a large laser gun crammed into a tank was able to shoot down an airplane and a helicopter. But the laser was so heavy that it made moving the tank difficult. And it also had a tendency to overheat and break down. So the project was cancelled.

In 1982, a weaker laser gun was developed that could not pierce through metal but could be directed over the enemy positions, blinding the soldiers. Actually, the soldiers would not really be blinded since they would certainly wear laser-proof goggles. But wearing those goggles reduces their vision. For example, laser-proof goggles make it hard for soldiers to distinguish camouflage green from natural green.

At present, some modern U.S. tanks are equipped with 20-pound lasers that guide bombs. A laser beam is bounced off an enemy target. The light reflected off the target is picked up by a telescope that sends the image to a computer. The computer analyzes that light and provides information that helps the cannon hit its mark. For example, it estimates how far away the target is, the speed and direction of the wind, the speed and direction the target is moving, and the humidity. The computer then aims the cannon in the right direction and sets it off. All this happens in less than one second.

Besides providing information about the enemy, lasers also can give an enemy false information about our positions. By directing a laser at enemy radar, it can create false readings.

And finally, lasers soon may be used to communicate with submarines. At present, subs must tow large antennas in order to pick up radio communication while submerged. But lasers from satellites can penetrate the water and communicate with the submarine.

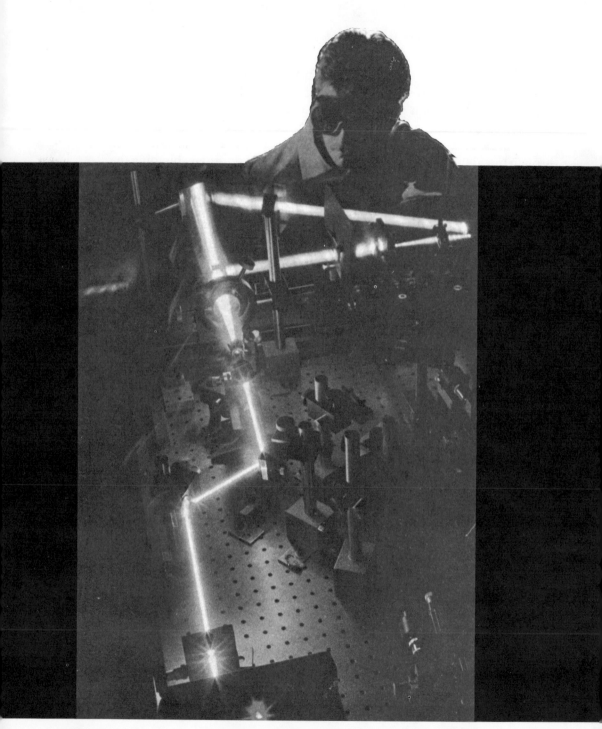

MAKING A HOLOGRAM.

5 | Holograms: Pictures That Come Alive

Someday this might happen:

You come home from school and flick on your favorite TV program. The show is about space travelers who fly around the galaxy bringing peace to warring planets. As your program comes on, you walk into the kitchen for a snack. When you return, your entire living room seems to be filled with asteroids, planets, and spaceships chasing each other.

Then the scene changes. People are walking along a busy street. But they seem to be in your living room.

Carrying your snack, you walk through the street scene. It is like a ghost. It has no substance. You sit in your favorite chair to watch the drama that is taking place in your living room.

No, this is not a witch's spell or a projection from an alien planet. It is a hologram, a three-dimensional image that can be projected in midair.

You may be familiar with 3-D movies or comic books, for which you wear special glasses to give the impression that the picture has depth. Three-dimensional pictures are made by drawing a double image. When you wear the special glasses, one image is invisible to your right eye, the other to your left eye. When you see both images together, the picture seems to have depth.

A hologram is quite different. With a hologram, you actually see depth. That is, you can see the picture from different angles: the front, the sides, even sometimes the back. Seeing a hologram image is almost like seeing the real thing.

The inventor of holography (the study of holograms) was a Hungarian Nobel Prize-winning scientist named Dennis Gabor. Recently, a visitor to CBS Labs in Stamford, Connecticut, walked past an open office where he saw Dr. Gabor looking out at him. "Good morning, sir!" said the visitor smiling, and then he continued on. But a few seconds later the visitor stopped in his tracks. He realized that Gabor could not have been in that room. He had died in 1979! The visitor stepped back to the open door and found the same smiling face. Whatever it is, it had not moved; the expression had not changed. Stepping into the room, the visitor realized that it was not Gabor at all but a very lifelike holographic image of him floating in the middle of the room.

Making a hologram is a very complicated process. But put very simply, it is created by intersecting laser beams. One beam comes out of the laser and is split into two with a lens. One of the two beams is bounced off the object being photographed and is reflected back onto photographic film. The other beam from the laser hits the photographic film directly without bouncing off the subject.

Since the laser beam hits many angles of the subject, the film is able to portray the subject from many angles. But if you look at the film without a laser, the image looks like a smudge. In order to see the image clearly, the film must be illuminated with a laser that unscrambles the image.

You may be familiar with holograms that can be seen in ordinary light without a laser. They are sometimes found on credit cards or stickers or even greeting cards. They are usually made of paper or plastic. If viewed from a certain angle in good light, they seem to be three-dimensional.

These holograms are created with lasers but they can be seen with ordinary white light. They are different from those that must be illuminated by lasers in order to be seen. Although they are three-dimensional, they don't really appear to be alive or floating in midair. The reason has to do with the difference between laser light and ordinary white light.

Laser light, as mentioned in Chapter 1, contains only one wavelength. White light has light waves of different lengths. They create the rainbow when white light is filtered through a prism. The different wavelengths in white light bend at different angles. But for a hologram to be seen, the image has to be bent at one angle only. A hologram viewed with white light seems like a colorful blur. The only way to make a hologram that can be seen under white light is to eliminate some of the angles of the image. So when you look at these holograms, you usually can see only two or three angles of the image.

Like laser technology in general, holography is a young science. As the years go by, however, scientists will discover new uses for it.

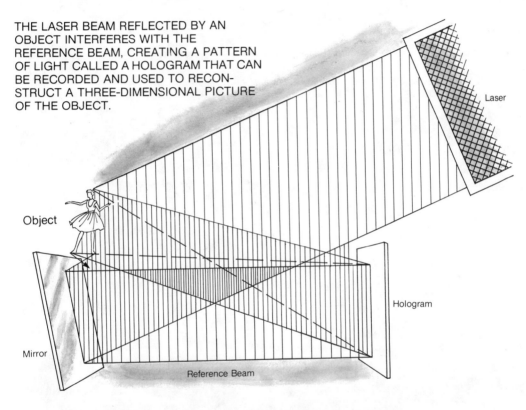

THE LASER BEAM REFLECTED BY AN OBJECT INTERFERES WITH THE REFERENCE BEAM, CREATING A PATTERN OF LIGHT CALLED A HOLOGRAM THAT CAN BE RECORDED AND USED TO RECON-STRUCT A THREE-DIMENSIONAL PICTURE OF THE OBJECT.

Laser

Object

Hologram

Mirror

Reference Beam

Certainly, having a hologram machine in your living room, as we envisioned at the beginning of this chapter, would be one of the most exciting uses of this science. Unfortunately, that probably won't be possible for many years. Most likely, holographic movies (some people call them "roundies") may first be available in theaters. But eventually, it is likely that scientists will discover ways to produce lasers and hologram machines that are inexpensive enough for almost everyone to own.

But holography is not only a technology for the future. Many people already have found interesting ways to put it to use.

32 SINCE HOLOGRAMS CANNOT BE ALTERED THEY ARE OFTEN USED
ON DOCUMENTS AND MONEY TO PREVENT FORGERY. HERE ARE
SOME BANK NOTES THAT USE HOLOGRAMS.

In the Soviet Union, for example, holographic pictures of sculptures and other works of art are taken to the countryside. People who live far from cities and museums are able to see these statutes and paintings as if they were really in front of them.

Another use is in aviation. When pilots land large planes, they often have to switch their gaze back and forth from the instrument gauges to the ground. Now, using holograms, the gauges can appear floating in front of the pilots' eyes. The images are clear enough to read but also are transparent enough to allow the pilot to look through them to the ground.

Like lasers, holograms also are helping at the checkout counter in grocery stores. Have you ever seen the laser readers at grocery checkout counters? The clerk passes the grocery item over a lens and the cash register rings up the item. But sometimes the clerk doesn't hold the package just right and the machine cannot read it. The clerk has to pass the grocery item over the lens again and again. Now a new machine designed by IBM has a holographic lens that can search out the bar codes and read them even if they are not positioned correctly.

Holography also is being used in industry to find tiny flaws, or mistakes, in pipes and other machine parts. A holographic picture of the part is taken. The hologram is then projected onto the part. Next, air is pumped into the pipe until tiny breaks appear. Without a hologram, those breaks could not be seen with the naked eye. But the breaks bend the hologram and form bull's-eyes where the breaks are.

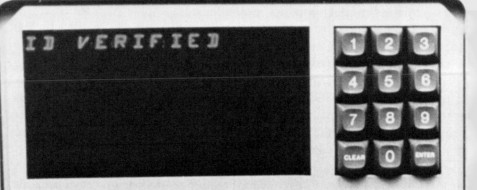

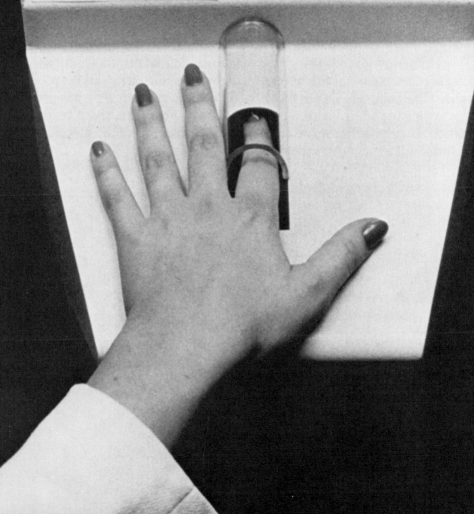

6 | Laser Locks: A Key That Is Always at Your Fingertips

You are a computer expert with the U.S. Defense Intelligence Agency. As you walk through the cavernous halls toward the computer room, you notice a man walking twenty yards ahead of you. He does not look familiar—perhaps he is a new employee. But you are a bit suspicious. This is, after all, one of the most sensitive rooms in the Pentagon. Any foreign spy who is able to get into the computer room would find volumes of valuable information.

Unauthorized people are prevented from entering the computer room through a complex series of checks. Up ahead, the man is about to go through one of the checkpoints. He inserts his identification card in a slot, then he punches in his secret identification number in a number pad next to the door. A computer matches the identification number that is encoded on his card with the number he punches in. If they match, the door will unlock and he will be able to pass through.

You hear a buzzer sound, which means the door is unlocking. And the man walks through. But he could have stolen the identification card. And he might have forced its owner to tell him the secret identification number. But you are not worried. If the man is a spy, he will never be able to pass through the second door.

When the man approaches the second door, he seems a bit confused and hesitant. He turns as if changing his mind about entering, but seeing you, he thinks better of it. He then puts his identification card in the slot. On a small computer screen these words appear: PLACE YOUR RIGHT INDEX FINGER ON THE PLASTIC PLATE.

AN INDIVIDUAL PRESENTS A FINGER FOR SCANNING BY THE FINGERMATRIX RIDGE READER.

A NAVY OFFICER PRESENTS A FINGER FOR SCANNING TO GAIN
ACCESS TO A SENSITIVE COMPUTER FACILITY.

After he complies, these words appear: PLACE YOUR RIGHT
THUMB ON THE PLASTIC PLATE.

He obeys. But less than one second later, a concealed door behind
the man slams shut, confining him. A loud bell goes off. And soon five
security guards come and take him away.

The spy was caught by a laser lock that reads fingerprints. When he
placed his finger on the plate, a weak laser illuminated it, casting shadows
on the ridges and valleys of his finger. Those shadows were compared with

those on file in the computer's memory. Since they didn't match, the computer signaled that the man was an imposter and the door was locked behind him.

This scene is not real. Few people know what happens in the Defense Intelligence Agency corridors. But it is known that the agency bought a number of these "personal touch verification" locks to test out. The reason is that it may be the most foolproof identification system available. As the president of a company that makes fingerprint locks said, "We are building a new kind of key, one that is better than the metal variety. Locks can be picked, but the ridges and valleys on a person's finger are uniquely his own and cannot be duplicated or stolen.

The "key" of a personal touch verification system is made by having a person enter his fingerprint into a computer. He does this by pressing his finger on a one-inch-square piece of plastic. The plastic "gives" a bit under his finger. This causes shadows to form as laser light scans his finger. The shadows are entered into the computer's memory. This memory then allows the person's fingerprint to become his key.

AN OFFICE WORKER QUICKLY LEARNS TO USE THE RIDGE READER
TO GAIN ACCESS TO SENSITIVE COMPUTER DATA.

Besides providing security for top secret areas, fingerprint locks may soon be used in other situations. For example, hotels have a problem when they issue keys to guests. Some people may take the keys with them when they check out and then return later to burglarize the room. It would be much safer to make a fingerprint key when the guest checks in and change it as soon as he or she checks out.

Sometimes in large companies people who are allowed to use the computer are not allowed to get certain information from the computer. For example, an accountant should be allowed to get information about the profits of the company. But he or she should not be allowed to access the personnel files where personal information about employees is stored. One solution is to have the person press a finger to a fingerprint lock before using the computer. That tells the computer what information that person is allowed to access.

Further in the future, laser fingerprint locks may be even more common than ordinary ones. They may be found in apartments, houses, automobiles, prisons, even some schools. You may never have to carry a metal key. The tips of your fingers may be all you need!

7 | Recording With Laser Beams

In 1877, Thomas Edison wrapped tinfoil around a metal cylinder. As the cylinder rotated, someone talked into a megaphone-type instrument. The vibrations from the speech were transferred to a needle. The needle then made grooves of different depths on the foil. Later a needle was dragged through the tracks, reproducing the sound. This process is sometimes called hill-and-valley recording.

The quality of records has improved greatly since the scratchy, barely audible record that Edison invented. But the process of hill-and-valley recording has remained basically the same. And even the best sound systems have limitations. For example, the range between the softest and loudest sounds is not the same as in a live performance. Also, slight changes in the speed that the turntable spins cause wavering of the music. Dust and scratches also detract from the quality. And even the best stylus causes the records to wear down a little after each use.

A new technology called digital disc (or compact disc) recording uses lasers and eliminates many of these problems. It also provides new features that were never possible before.

LASER DISC PORTABLE CD PLAYER.

A tiny laser beam, finer than a human hair, emitted from a device about the size of a grain of sand, hits the face of a metal disc. The disc, which spins at from 200 to 500 rotations per minute (RPM), appears bright and polished. But actually it contains millions of microscopic pits and flat areas. As the laser beam hits those areas, it reflects back a different image based on the shape of the pit or flat area. That image is translated into computer code. There are 65,000 possible codes that are in turn translated into notes or other sounds.

Sixty-five thousand different sounds is a lot more than possible with conventional recordings. The sound from compact discs is therefore more brilliant, more true to life. There is no background noise, distortion, or variation in pitch.

Besides better sound quality, compact disc recorders can have other interesting features. For example, you can program them to play only certain songs, and play them in the order you choose. And soon, discs will be available that contain visual information such as notes, still photographs, or librettos. You will be able to listen to music and see the notes flash on a screen. Or you can listen to a foreign opera and simultaneously see the English translation.

To record music, a compact disc converts sound into numbers that can be read by a tiny computer housed in the player. Sound travels in waves that can be measured. To record a compact disc, computers measure sound waves 44,100 times each second. These wavelengths are translated into computer code and then into a puncture, or pit, on the disc. Each disc has a two-and-one-half-mile track of pits.

Compact discs also can hold movies, but since they cannot record, most people have chosen to buy video cassette recorders instead. Soon, though, compact disc players may be able to erase and record. When this happens, the possibilities available on these machines may make them more popular than video cassette recorders.

One of the most important features of compact discs is their ability to jump around, picking out images anyplace on the disc. That will allow a new type of movie called interactive movie to be created. At various places in the movie you will be asked how you would like the movie to progress. For example, should the hero chase the fleeing gunman, call for help, or run for cover? Your choice decides which way the movie will unfold.

Recently, scientists at Massachusetts Institute of Technology created a video map of Aspen, Colorado. They took 54,000 pictures of the city and placed them on a videodisc. When connected to a computer, you can use that videodisc to take a "ride" through Aspen. As you turn left or right and wander through the streets of Aspen, you see the roads, buildings, stores, and parks that are really there.

The National Air and Space Museum at the Smithsonian Institution is offering a ten-disc set of its entire collection of photos on aviation. At $30, each disc contains 50,000 photos. You can view in your home rare photos of the Wright brothers, Charles Lindbergh, and Amelia Earhart. Another disc, published by Videodisc Publishing Co., Inc., offers a tour of the National Gallery of Art.

Videodiscs are still rare, and that has discouraged many people from buying videodisc players. Audio discs are a bit more available, but they too are relatively rare. There are fewer than 1,000 titles available. About half of them are pop; about 40 percent, classical; and the rest, jazz and rock. They are also expensive—about $20 a disc. The players are also expensive—about $700 each. But, as with color TVs, calculators, and computers, the price of compact disc equipment is expected to drop quickly. Many people expect it to drop to about $350 in 1986 and to around $200 in 1987. When prices fall and when they are able to record as well as play back, it is likely that these laser recorders will replace conventional recording and playing devices.

8 | Laser Safety Hazards

Lasers present certain safety hazards that have never been experienced before. As they become more common in factories, hospitals, in the military, and other places, people will have to get used to taking new types of safety precautions.

The body organ that is most sensitive to laser radiation is the eye. That is because the function of this organ is to focus light; and when light is focused, it becomes stronger. The light intensity that hits the cornea at the front of the eyeball may be increased several hundred thousand times by the focusing power of the eye. For that reason, it is much more dangerous to look directly at a laser beam than to see it at the corner of your eye.

A vivid firsthand account of what laser radiation can do to the eye is given by laser physicist C. David Decker in a magazine called *Laser Focus*. One day, Dr. Decker was working with a laser in his lab when, accidentally, the beam hit his eye.

He writes: "When the beam struck my eye I heard a distinct popping sound caused by a laser-induced explosion at the back of my eyeball. My vision was obscured almost immediately by streams of blood floating in the vitreous humor. There was a local pain within a few minutes of the accident, but it did not become excruciating. The most immediate response after such an accident is horror. As a Vietnam War veteran, I have seen several terrible scenes of human carnage, but none affected me more than viewing the world through my bloodfilled eyeball."

Although Dr. Decker was not blinded from this accident, he did sustain some permanent damage to his eye and lost some vision.

To protect against this danger, laser filters can be put into glass frames, goggles, and windows.

Next to the eye, the skin and organs lying close to the skin are most in danger from laser radiation. To protect the skin, heavy white cloth, which reflects rather than absorbs light, is best. Gloves also should be worn. Also, laser equipment should have shields that protect users from coming in contact with beams.

And finally, some laser activities will cause poisonous gases to be released. Proper venting and breathing devices can prevent accidents in this area.

It is important to understand that these safety problems involve the use of lasers in military, experimental, and factory situations. Lasers that are used in the home or in areas where the public is invited have proven to be extremely safe.

9 | Is a Career in Lasers for You?

If you find lasers exciting, you might consider making a career in this fast-growing field. Of course, working with lasers probably won't mean you will spend your time playing with light guns or putting on light shows. You may be working more with numbers and diagrams than with machines. But you will have the satisfaction of knowing you are contributing to one of the most important technologies of this century—perhaps of all time.

If you do choose to enter this field, you will find plenty of opportunities for employment. The Federal Bureau of Labor Statistics reports that laser-related jobs are among the nation's fastest growing professions. Jobs in this area will grow from 25 to 50 percent faster than jobs in other areas.

Although lasers were discovered 25 years ago, products that use lasers are only now being put on sale. About 25 percent more laser products were sold this year than last year. And next year, sales of lasers should grow another 25 percent or more.

Since the use of lasers has increased so rapidly, there is a shortage of people who know how to work with them. And still, very few schools have programs that train laser technicians or scientists. So there is a shortage of laser workers that is likely to last many years—at least until 1992 and perhaps until the end of the century. So when you are ready to enter the work force, there will still be a strong need for people who understand lasers. And that means there will still be plenty of rewarding and well-paying jobs to choose from.

At present, there are two ways you can enter the laser field.

You can be a laser engineer or scientist. If you choose this type of work, you will be helping develop, design, and invent laser equipment. You will need a college degree in physics or electrical engineering. You will be studying lasers during your time at college, but no college now offers special degrees in laser physics or engineering. Once you get your degree, you will likely be hired by a company that makes laser machinery, and you will be trained on the job.

Many people consider the work required for a degree in physics or engineering to be difficult. You will need to be good in science and math. But if you complete your course, you will find yourself doing very exciting and important laser work. And your salary will reflect your importance. Salaries for laser scientists now start at about $35,000 to $40,000 a year.

A second way to get into the laser field is to be a laser technician. Laser technicians install, build, and repair laser equipment. You will not be designing or inventing laser machines like a laser scientist, but you will have more hands-on experience with lasers.

Studying to be a laser technician is easier than studying to be a laser scientist. You will need to go to a school that offers courses in laser technology. Currently, finding such a school near you may not be easy. There are only 27 of them around the country. But by the time you are ready for it, the number of schools offering laser programs will likely increase.

Laser technicians do not earn as much as laser scientists. Presently, they start at about $18,000 to $25,000 a year. But many laser technicians gradually work their way up to become laser scientists. In fact, a laser expert at General Electric, Inc., said that laser technicians who later become laser scientists are often better at their jobs than those who get degrees in physics or engineering.

By the time you are ready to choose a career, there may be other ways to get into the laser field. For example, the Armed Forces will be needing laser technicians. So they may very well offer it as a job classification for you to choose. And the many factories that use laser machines will need people to run them.

Laser technology will have many facets. We are only on the threshold of its development and future uses. One day in the future, *you* may offer the world new insights and new uses of lasers never dreamed of before.

Glossary

Coherent light: light, such as laser light, made up of waves of the same length.

Continuous wave laser: a weapon that stays on target until it bores a hole in it.

Electrons: parts of an atom that let off energy when stimulated.

Hologram: a three dimensional image made possible with lasers.

Interactive movie: a movie made possible by lasers that allow the viewer to change the action.

Laser machinery: a drill, cutting tool, welding tool or other machine that uses a laser to perform its function.

Nonintrusive surgery: surgery that is done with lasers instead of knives.

Personal touch verification system: a laser lock that opens when an authorized person touches it.

Photon: a quantity of radiation.

Pulsed laser: a weapon that delivers short powerful "hits" at the target.

Vaporize: to turn a substance into a gas, as many laser machines do.

Watt: a measurement of power.

Wavelength: the measurement of a wave of light.

INDEX